HOW IT HAPPENED

SNEAKERS

The Cool Stories and Facts

Behind Every Pair

10025184

HOW iT HAPPENED

SNEAKERS

The Cool Stories and Facts
Behind Every Pair

BY STEPHANIE WARREN DRIMMER

ILLUSTRATED BY DAN SIPPLE

union
square
kids

NEW YORK

union
square
kids

NEW YORK

UNION SQUARE KIDS and the distinctive Union Square Kids
logo are trademarks of Union Square & Co., LLC.

Union Square & Co., LLC, is a subsidiary
of Sterling Publishing Co., Inc.

ISBN 978-1-4549-4496-6 (hardcover)
ISBN 978-1-4549-4512-3 (paperback)
ISBN 978-1-4549-4597-3 (e-book)

Library of Congress Control Number: 2022942717

For information about custom editions, special sales,
and premium purchases, please contact
specialsales@unionsquareandco.com.

Printed in Malaysia

Lot #:
2 4 6 8 10 9 7 5 3 1

12/22

unionsquareandco.com

Cover design by Whitney Manger and Liam Donnelly
Cover art by Becca Clason
Interior illustrations and series logo by Dan Sipple
Interior design by Nicole Lazarus
Created and produced by WonderLab Group, LLC
Photo research by Kelley Miller
Fact-checked by Annika Robbins
Sensitivity review by Nina Tsang
Copyedited by Molly Reid
Indexed by Connie Binder
Proofread by Susan Hom
Image credits—see page 192

Table of Contents

What is the Last Thing You Do Before You Leave the House Every Morning?

Do you pack your bag, check your phone, or snuggle your pet goodbye? Whether you do all or none of these things, your morning routine probably involves pulling on shoes. And unless you're heading to the beach or trudging through the snow, chances are those shoes are a pair of *sneakers*!

Sneaker fans exist everywhere, from Hollywood to the NBA. But humans

weren't always wearing sneakers—in fact, they weren't always wearing shoes at all. How did we go from running barefoot in the grass to stomping around in rubber-soled lace-ups? The answer will take you on a journey through the rubber tree plantations of Southeast Asia, the dark days of Nazi Germany, the parks of New York City, and more. Get ready to step into the ins and outs of a shoe that has influenced sports, music, fashion, and more. It's time to find out how the sneaker became the worldwide phenomenon it is today!

SECTION ONE

How It All Started

CHAPTER ONE

The Dawn of Rubber

Sneakers Get Going

It might be hard to imagine a world without shoes, just as it's hard to imagine a world without clothes. But most ancient humans went around barefoot. Experts say that our feet and legs are perfectly built for running long distances. Some prehistoric people may have survived by outrunning antelope and other animals they hunted. They would chase their prey until it got too tired to keep going! And they performed this feat with bare feet.

A pair of 7,000-year-old sagebrush sandals

Oldest Shoe

In 1938, archaeologist Luther Cressman unearthed something extraordinary in Oregon's Fort Rock Cave: dozens of sandals woven out of a woody plant called sagebrush. The sandals turned out to be at least 9,000 years old, making them the oldest shoes ever discovered with a known date.

When a cook by the name of Koroibos won the 600-foot race in the world's first Olympic Games in ancient Greece, barefoot running was still the norm. Over time, athletes realized they could outperform the competition by donning sandals to protect their feet from rocks and hot sand. And ever since, footwear has been designed and redesigned to help athletes perform at their best.

But today's superstars might still be running in sandals if it wasn't for a curious substance hiding deep in the South American rain forest: rubber.

Rubber, Naturally

A sneaker isn't a sneaker without its rubber sole. But what exactly is rubber, and how is it made?

Believe it or not, rubber has been around since ancient times. Rubber plants and trees grow in warm tropical areas around the world, such as South America and Southeast Asia. When you cut into their stems and trunks, the plants and trees ooze out a milky, sap-like fluid called latex (pronounced LAY-tecks). Over time, the latex turns into a hard, sticky material.

The Indigenous peoples living 3,000 years ago in Mesoamerica—such as the Aztec,

Morning glory

Maya, and Olmec—were rubber experts. They tapped into rubber trees to drain out the latex. Then they mixed the latex with the juice from morning glory vines, which created a white material that was stretchy and bouncy. By mixing varying amounts of the two substances together, they could make different kinds of rubber ideal for different purposes.

Experts believe ancient Indigenous people created durable rubber to craft shoes. After molding chunks of clay into the shape of their feet, they would pour the latex mixture over the molds. Then, they would place the latex-covered mold in the coals of a fire, where the latex would harden into something a bit like a rubber slipper.

Latex is tapped from the trunk of a rubber tree.

Rubber Barons

Indigenous peoples in the Amazon were also early rubber users. When French explorers arrived in the 1700s, they were fascinated by the Indigenous people's rubber creations. Dreaming of growing rich from rubber products, the French explorers named the material caoutchouc (pronounced COW-chook) and brought samples back home with them. A British scientist realized that the material worked well for erasing pencil marks if you rubbed it against paper . . . and that's how the word "rubber" was born!

A rubber fever took hold in Europe and North America in the early 1800s, and demand for the stuff soared. People in the United States figured out how to turn rubber into crude

An ancient Maya pitz court

Bouncy Balls

Some ancient Maya people used rubber to make bouncy balls. Pitz, an ancient Maya ball game, was a bit like a cross between modern soccer and basketball. Players would bounce a rubber ball through stone hoops attached to the sides of a court but without using their hands. Pitz was incredibly important to ancient Maya society. Pitz courts were located at the center of town and covered in murals showing wars, myths, and the passage of power from one ruler to another. Rather than fighting on the battlefield, neighboring cities would use pitz games to settle disputes. Sometimes, the Maya people would even make a human sacrifice from the losing team at the end of the game.

galoshes to protect their shoes from water and mud. Inventors tried making all kinds of other things out of rubber, too, like coats, hats, and life preservers.

Rubber barons moved into small towns along the Amazon River and took over. They brought in private armies who captured

The Amazon River runs through Brazil, Colombia, and Peru.

Indigenous people and claimed their land. They enslaved the people, forcing them to work on rubber plantations on the land where they and their families had lived for generations.

Meanwhile, the rubber barons lived like kings. Despite the horrible acts committed in the name of rubber, no Western people knew how to use it successfully for a very long time. It would take the persistence of one dreamer and entrepreneur named Charles Goodyear to change that.

Good Call, Goodyear

You might recognize the name Goodyear from car tires or the side of a blimp at sports events. But Charles Goodyear didn't start out as a brilliant businessman who would have a company named in his honor. In fact, he spent time behind bars when his

> ## "The ball made thereof, though hard and heavy to the hand, did bound and fly as well as our footballs, there being no need to blow them."
>
> **—18TH-CENTURY SPANISH EXPLORER ANTONIO DE HERRERA, DESCRIBING AN AZTEC GAME WITH A RUBBER BALL**

family hardware business failed in 1830 and he couldn't pay back his debts.

Goodyear decided he was done selling products other people had created. Instead, he was going to invent one for himself. And he knew exactly what material he was going to use to make his new creation: rubber.

In 1834, 33-year-old Goodyear was strolling along a New York City street when he spotted a rubber life preserver in a store window. Something about it made him stop short. It had a shoddy valve, and Goodyear knew he could design a better one. A few weeks of tinkering and he had the finished product: a leak-proof valve. Here it was, his million-dollar idea!

Except it wasn't. When Goodyear took his newly

designed valve to the store, the salesman led him to a nearby warehouse and showed him the real problem: shelves upon shelves filled with rubber blobs that had once been life preservers. The salesman explained that rubber had a fatal flaw. It melted in the heat and turned brittle and cracked in the cold. After one hot summer, the life preservers were ruined forever.

Goodyear's valve was useless. But by designing one failed product, he had stumbled onto a better idea: to find a way to keep rubber stable in changing temperatures. If Goodyear could crack that code, he would hold the secret to making rubber into all kinds of products. He bought the warehouse full of ruined life preservers and set to work.

Goodyear tried everything he could think of. He mixed different chemicals into the rubber. He baked it in the sun. But nothing worked. Finally, in 1839, he had an accidental breakthrough when he was visiting a store in Woburn, Massachusetts. While trying to convince the owner to buy some of his rubber, Goodyear swung his arm to make a gesture and accidentally sent a lump of rubber flying onto the hot surface of a potbellied stove. When Goodyear scraped the rubber off the stove, he noticed that the normally soft rubber had hardened.

It took five more years of experimenting. Goodyear ran so low on money that he pawned his furniture for cash. He even landed back in jail because he couldn't pay his debts. But he kept on working, and even continued his experiments while in prison! At last, his years of work paid off: Goodyear discovered that by adding sulfur to the rubber and getting it hot enough, he could create a durable material. This material could be formed into just about anything without cracking or melting.

Goodyear named the new process **vulcanization** after Vulcan, the Roman god of fire. He dreamed of a future where everything from musical instruments to clothes would be made of rubber.

Unfortunately, rubbermakers around the world stole Goodyear's idea and started making their own vulcanized rubber products. Instead of cashing in on his invention, Goodyear spent the rest of his life trying to protect it. He died in 1860, still in debt.

But Goodyear's creation changed the world. While he didn't found the Goodyear Tire & Rubber Company, the business was named in his honor in 1898. Vulcanized rubber completely changed how products are made, from bicycle tires to car parts—and sneakers, of course.

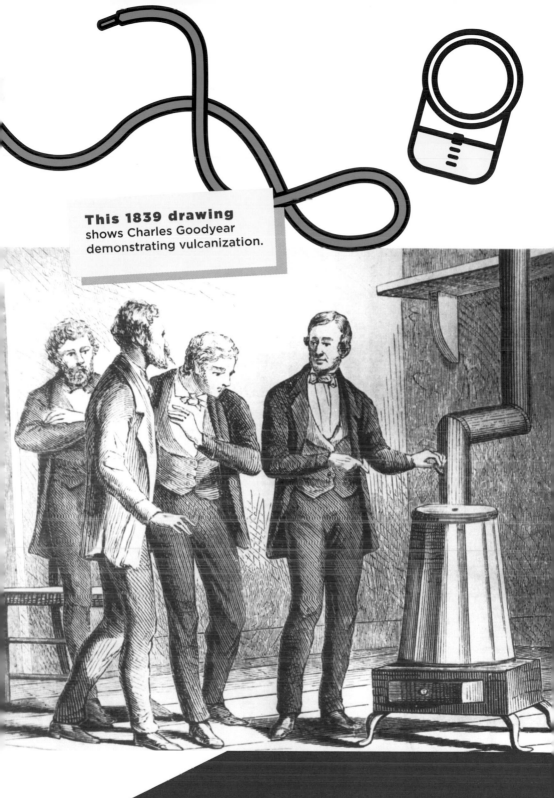

This 1839 drawing shows Charles Goodyear demonstrating vulcanization.

The Goodyear Tire & Rubber Company currently owns four blimps. They use them to advertise their company and record footage at sports events.

CHAPTER TWO

Good for the Sole

Fun in the Sun

Until the 1800s, only the wealthy could take vacations. Most people grew their own food, sewed their own clothes, and even made their own shoes. But with the Industrial Revolution and the rise of technology, all that changed. For the first time, many goods were made in factories.

People left their farms and moved into the cities to work. (Some of them even worked in factories that manufactured rubber products.)

Many people worked long hours under dangerous conditions. But for one week each year, factories would shut down so that the machines could be inspected and repaired. With their paychecks in their pockets and a week of free time, the new working class often headed for the beach.

People frolicked on the shores—or they tried to, anyway. It's not easy to frolic in work boots, the only kind of footwear most people had. Soon a new type of shoe sprouted up. Cheap sand shoes were made of canvas with a sole made of cork or rope. They were great for strolling on the beach. But if you tried to splash in the waves, the shoes would become a soggy mess.

Running in Heels

Ouch! Have you ever run in shoes that weren't meant for running? Chances are you didn't get too far before your feet started to hurt. The earliest known running shoe must not have been very comfortable. It looks like a dress shoe made of smooth black leather. It even has a small heel! The only clues that the shoe was intended for athletics were a band of leather across the top, which added support, and spikes on the heel and toe, which helped the wearer dig into the ground and gain speed. Imagine running in that!

These running shoes from the 1800s are a far cry from athletic sneakers today!

In 1832, a New Yorker named Wait Webster came one step closer to lacing up the connection between rubber and shoes. He replaced the sole on sand shoes with rubber. These rubber soles had the same problem as the original rubber life preservers, though—they would melt in the summer heat. Once Goodyear cracked the method of vulcanized rubber, the canvas and rubber shoes began to take off.

It's Game Time!

While people loved going to the beach, they also looked for other ways to have a little fun. They turned their attention to something that was beginning to boom in popularity: sports!

Various forms of sports have been around for thousands of years. In the 1800s, though, new technology helped fuel the rise of sports to a whole new level. Trains could transport athletes to sporting venues, and streetcars could carry their fans to watch the games. Light bulbs could illuminate indoor sporting arenas, which meant athletes could play after the sun set. And the invention of the telegraph and telephone meant that the outcome could be reported quickly to faraway cities.

The first major professional sports were baseball, boxing, and horse racing. Other sports were catching on, too. **Croquet** (pronounced krow-KAY) became extremely popular in the 1850s and 1860s. Both men and women were allowed on the croquet field, which was unusual for sporting events at the time. The sport became a big hit with young people especially.

And these casual competitors wanted to look their best while they played, but they found that their fashionable white shoes would quickly become covered with grass stains from the croquet court. They needed a shoe with a sole made of stain-resistant material. And lightweight canvas sand shoes—complete with a durable rubber sole—were the perfect answer.

There are many variations to croquet, like association croquet and golf croquet.

Make a Break!

To win in a game of croquet, you must hit the balls through hoops and pegs faster than your opponent. You can play with just two people or in larger teams. Croquet shares some similarities with golf and miniature golf—you play on a grassy lawn and use a long mallet to hit the ball.

The First Sneaker Brand

By the end of the nineteenth century, America was rubber crazy. Manufacturers were churning out rubber bicycle tires, rubber car parts such as belts and hoses, and, of course, rubber shoes. Different manufacturers sold shoes under different names until 1916, when the U.S. Rubber Company gathered all of them under a single name: Peds, named after the Latin word for feet. When the company realized that—oops!—that name was already trademarked, they changed one letter and launched Keds.

Champion, the first shoe released by Keds, was a white canvas high-top. People wore Keds shoes not just for croquet, but for all kinds of sports, such as tennis.

Since both men and women played tennis, Keds began advertising to women as well as men. In 1924, the company ran an advertisement in *Boy's Life* magazine boasting that the sneakers were ideal for climbing trees and playing baseball. Four years later, it ran an ad in a girls' magazine with the same message: Keds would help girls run faster and climb higher. In 1930, it even released a line of shoes just for women. Called Kedettes, they were

A Keds ad from the mid-1900s

Summertime U.S.A. begins with U.S. KEDS...for everybody

US United States Rubber

> ## "Once a novel experiment—today a national habit."
>
> **—KEDS ADVERTISEMENT FROM THE 1920S**

washable canvas sneakers—with a high heel! Keds advertised that they were just as comfortable as a regular sneaker.

The idea of selling shoes for women isn't surprising today. But when the Keds company was formed, women couldn't vote, join the military, or do many other things that men could do. It was groundbreaking for a company to target both men and women. Not to mention that they advertised a shoe to encourage girls to run and climb,

Early female tennis players wore high-heeled boots, along with long-sleeved tops and skirts that reached their ankles.

Tennis player **Helen Wills** competes on the court at Wimbledon, London.

contradicting the social pressure at the time for girls to be calm and proper, which meant not being physically active.

Keds also became the shoe of choice for tennis players. In the 1924 Olympics, American tennis players won every single tennis medal, and all of them did it wearing Keds. In the 1920s and 1930s, female tennis phenomenon Helen Wills dominated the sport, winning 31 major international tennis championships. On the court, she wore—you guessed it—Keds.

Tennies and Plimsolls and Sneakers, Oh My!

Over time, croquet slipped out of fashion. But the rubber-soled shoes were here to stay. In Britain, they were called plimsolls, a name that came from the "plimsoll lines" painted on the side of a ship to show how low it was in the water. In the United States, they were called tennis shoes, tennies, or sometimes, sneakers.

No one is sure where the name "sneakers" came from. Until recently, the Keds company claimed that an advertising agent coined the term for their product in 1917. Keds claimed that he called the rubber-soled shoes "sneakers" because they allowed the wearer to walk without making noise and sneak up on someone who wasn't expecting them. Experts have since confirmed that the term came decades earlier than Keds, but they're

still not exactly sure where the word comes from. Some people think baseball players, who found the shoes perfect for stealing bases, coined the term. Others say that it was a nickname kids used because they could quietly sneak up on people and play pranks.

No matter who first thought it up, the name stuck around!

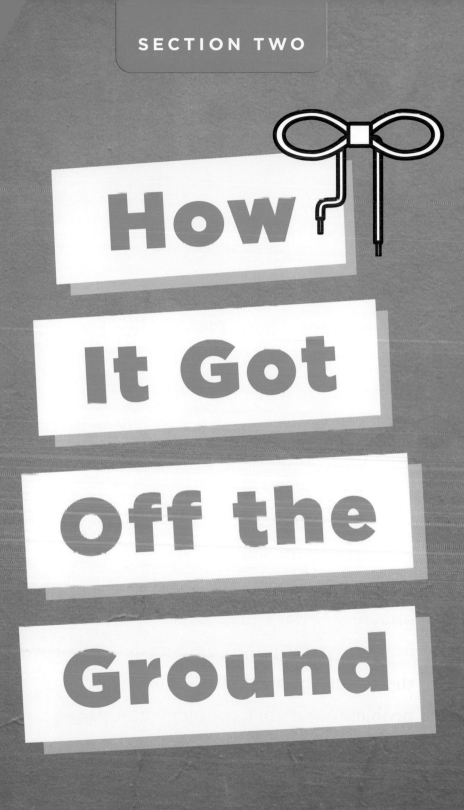

How It Got Off the Ground

CHAPTER THREE

A Good Rivalry

Run, Run, Run

When runner Jesse Owens dug his shoes into the dirt track at the 1936 Olympic Games, there was more than just a medal on the line. Owens was about to race in Berlin's Olympic Stadium in Nazi Germany. German chancellor Adolf Hitler was scheming to use the Olympics to show the world that the German people belonged to a "master race" that made them superior to other humans. Hitler's plan was for the German athletes to crush the competition and prove their number-one status. But Hitler had a problem, and that problem was American track and field star Jesse Owens.

Jesse Owens

"*I let my feet spend as little time on the ground as possible. From the air, fast down, and from the ground, fast up.*"

—TRACK SUPERSTAR JESSE OWENS

At the time, Owens was the best runner in history. While he was still in high school, Owens tied the world record for the 100-yard dash. During one meet as a freshman at Ohio State University, Owens, who was struggling with a sore back after falling down a flight of stairs, tied another world record and set three new ones . . . all in the span of forty-five minutes.

All the while, Owens faced racial discrimination as a Black man. Though he was one of the top high school athletes, he wasn't given any college scholarships. He wasn't allowed to live on the Ohio State University campus with his teammates. When his team traveled for competitions, Owens had to eat at separate restaurants and stay in separate hotels. But this terrible

Jesse's full name was James Cleveland Owens. When he moved from Alabama to Ohio as a young boy, he introduced himself to his new teacher as "J. C." His teacher accidentally misheard it as "Jesse" and that's how he became known!

treatment didn't stop him from being the best he could be.

At the 1936 Olympics, as Hitler watched from the stands, Owens blew away the other runners from around the world, including Nazi Germany. He won gold medals in the 100-meter dash, the 200-meter dash, the 400-meter relay, and the broad jump (now known as the long jump). Owens didn't just win each event—he set or helped to set records in them all.

Owens's achievements were so spectacular that his four-medal Olympic record stood for nearly twenty years. As he sped to victory, he tore Hitler's master race theory apart. He also proved that individual talent and drive can lead to success, even under difficult circumstances.

And Owens did it all while wearing a pair of sneakers unlike anything that had been seen before.

A Sneaker for Every Sport

Jesse Owens may have beat out his German competitors, but there was one German who was thrilled to watch it happen: Adolf "Adi" Dassler, the maker of Owens's strange shoes. To Dassler, the Olympic Games was the chance he'd been waiting for to launch his shoe business.

Dassler was born in 1900 in a small town in southern Germany called Herzogenaurach. He had three older siblings, including an older brother named Rudolf. Their father, like most people in the town, made a living by working for one of the many shoe factories there.

Young Adi was apprenticed to be a baker, but his true passion was sports. He spent all his free time either watching or competing in soccer, ice hockey, and track and field. His background in shoes made him notice something: The athletes wore the same shoes no matter which sport they played. Surely, Adi thought, it would be better if they had shoes made specially for their sport.

In 1914, Adi's brother Rudolf left to fight in World War I. In 1918, Adi was drafted into the military, where he served until 1919. After his return, Adi converted his mother's laundry room into a shoe workshop to explore his idea of making different shoes for each sport.

With the war over, materials were in short supply. Even electricity in Germany was limited. But that didn't stop Adi. He rigged a bicycle frame to a leather-making machine and hired his first employee to power the machine by pedaling!

Adi's hard work paid off. When he sent samples of his shoes to sports clubs, orders

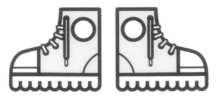

started pouring in. In 1923, Adi's older brother Rudolf joined his business, and they named their company Gebrüder Dassler Sportschuhfabrik (Dassler Brothers Sport Shoe Factory). Adi was the creative one, in charge of designing the shoes, and Rudolf oversaw the sales. Business was slow at first because people in Germany didn't have much money to spend after the war, but Adi and Rudolf kept at it. By the mid-1930s, the Dassler brothers were known across their country.

When the Dassler brothers heard that the Olympics were coming to Germany's capital city, Berlin, they saw an opportunity to catapult their company beyond Germany's borders. They just had to find a way to get one of the athletes to wear their shoes. In 1936, Adi put some of his track and field sneakers in a bag and headed for the Olympic

Village, where he caught sight of star runner Jesse Owens.

Adi spoke very little English, and Owens didn't speak German. But the shoes did the talking. They were low-cut and made of black leather, with two stripes along the outsides. The front of the sole had six handmade spikes that splayed outward to dig into the track better. Owens was very intrigued.

Owens liked the shoes so much that he went on to wear them for all four of his gold medal wins. And just as Adi and Rudolf had hoped, people noticed. After the Olympics was over, their shoe sales skyrocketed. Soon, the Dassler brothers were running multiple factories and making shoes for eleven different sports.

Falling Out

But then the Dassler brothers hit a major setback: World War II. In 1939, both brothers were required to report for the military draft. German athletics came to a standstill, and nobody was buying shoes. The brothers had to close a factory. In 1941, they were instructed to stop making sports shoes and start producing thousands of pairs of shoes for the German army. Then, as the German army began to fail, the Dassler factories were ordered to stop making shoes and manufacture spare tank parts and weapons instead.

The brothers butted heads over how to keep the company going. Their arguments grew more and more hostile. The war made things worse: While Adi was able to mostly stay out of

combat to run the company, Rudolf was drafted into the army.

Rudolf grew bitter and became convinced that Adi was plotting to get rid of him and gain full control of the company. Adi, on the other hand, thought Rudolf had a hand in forcing their factory to create weapons instead of shoes. Outraged by each other's actions, the brothers spilt the company in two in 1948. It was the last time they would ever speak.

Modern Adidas sneakers

Adi Dassler took over one surviving factory. He named his new company after himself—ADI DASsler became Adidas. Rudolf took over the other factory and named his new company Ruda, before changing it to the more athletic-sounding name Puma.

A pair of Pumas

The brothers didn't just want their company names to set them apart, but their designs as well. Adi decided that all Adidas shoes would have three parallel stripes on the outside. Puma shoes, Rudolf declared, would have a curving horizontal stripe. All it took was one glance to tell which brother's shoe someone was wearing.

When Rudolf Dassler founded Puma, the company only had fourteen employees. Today, they have more than ten thousand employees all over the world!

A Dark Past

Living in Germany after World War I wasn't easy. In 1933, Hitler took over the country as an all-powerful dictator. He led the Nazi Party, officially known as the National Socialist German Workers' Party, which conducted atrocities such as the murder of millions of people who they deemed "unfit" for society.

Under the Nazi regime, a German citizen could not stay neutral. You were either a party member, or you were against the party and risked your own safety. Rudolf and Adi joined the Nazi Party in the mid-1930s, a decision that supported the growth of their business.

The United States made posters that urged people to conserve rubber products.

CHAPTER FOUR
Synthetic Sneakers

Closed Borders

World War I and World War II profoundly affected the history of sneakers. It strained relations between the Dassler brothers and raised the stakes for athletes like Jesse Owens. It also changed what sneakers were made of . . . literally!

In the early 1900s, most rubber came from rubber tree plantations in Asia. American and European companies would use that natural material to make products like tires, water hoses, and sneakers. In fact, these companies couldn't get their hands on enough rubber to make all the products they wanted. Germany began researching ways to create rubber that was **synthetic** (pronounced sin-THET-ik), or made by humans.

In the early 1900s, factory workers made rubber shoes by hand.

In 1914, when World War I began, countries that had been trading materials and goods suddenly found their borders closed. Britain blocked Germany from its sources of natural rubber. Left with no good choices, Germany started mass-producing a synthetic rubber called methyl rubber. However, methyl rubber was both more expensive and of lesser quality than its natural counterpart.

In the mid-1920s, the United States was using more than three-quarters of the entire world's output of rubber.

Even after World War I, the price for natural rubber varied widely, sometimes reaching extraordinarily high rates. While demand for rubber continued to grow, many countries looked for better and cheaper ways to make rubber themselves.

United We Stand

When World War II started in 1939, the United States found themselves in a sticky situation. With the world at war, the nation suddenly lost 90 percent of its natural rubber sources coming in from abroad.

In 1940, President Franklin D. Roosevelt created the Rubber Reserve Company to help build America's synthetic rubber

industry. Putting competition aside in the name of war, different companies and researchers worked together to heat up the domestic rubber production. Patriotism and a collaborative spirit created a winning formula. In 1941, the United States made less than 9,000 tons of synthetic rubber. By 1945, they were making more than 915,000 tons!

By the mid-1950s, American rubber was split halfway between artificial and natural. Nowadays, synthetic rubber is cheaper, and almost all sneaker soles are made from the synthetic stuff.

The Anatomy of a Shoe

Despite their sleek design, sneakers are made of many complex parts working together. While there are dozens of different components, here are a few of the major ones:

The **upper** covers the top, sides, front, and back of your foot—in other words, everything but the bottom.

The **laces** make sure that the sneaker fits snugly and doesn't fall off your foot. Laces are woven through holes called **eyelets.**

The **tongue** is part of the upper, and it covers the top of your foot. It's a strip of fabric that sits in the middle of the shoe under the laces.

The **sole** is actually made of multiple parts. The **insole,** which you can only see from the inside of the shoe, makes direct contact with your foot. The **midsole,** which you can see from the outside, is the thick foam layer that cushions your foot. The **outsole** is the bottom-most layer that directly touches the ground.

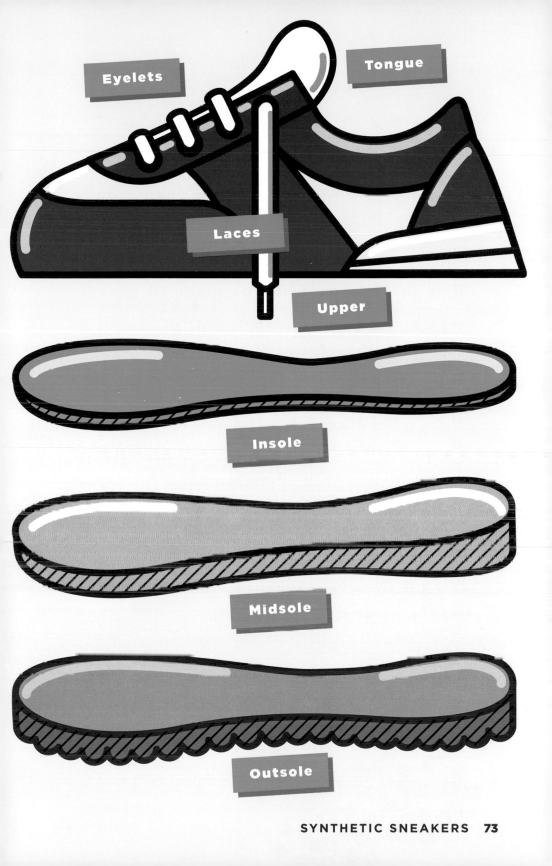

Cut from a Different Cloth

Around the same time that synthetic rubber soles replaced natural rubber soles, other sneaker materials were changing, too. The first sneakers had uppers made of canvas, which is typically woven cotton. Then, in 1965, Adidas broke ground by creating a tennis shoe made of leather. The white shoe was called the Adidas Robert Haillet, named after a French professional tennis player. When Haillet retired from the sport, Adidas found a new tennis player, and the leather sneaker took on the name it still has today: Stan Smith.

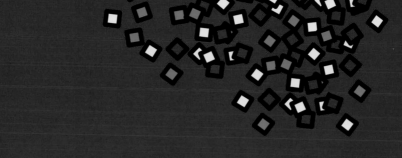

"Some people think I'm a shoe!"

—FORMER PROFESSIONAL TENNIS PLAYER STAN SMITH

The success of the Stan Smith inspired other companies to release their own versions of the leather sneaker. Other companies experimented with materials such as satin, suede, and synthetic fabrics like nylon.

As more sneaker styles made from different materials entered the market, athletes were spoiled for good choices. There was nothing "sneaky" about sneakers anymore. Whether you were serving on the tennis court or hitting the track, sneakers were the go-to athletic footwear.

WHAT DO YOU THINK?

Think of a time in your life when healthy competition helped you succeed, just like different companies pushed each other to make better sneakers. Maybe you donated the most cans at a food drive to win first prize, or you practiced harder to beat a rival team. Next, think of a time when working together led to an accomplishment, just like the Rubber Reserve Company collaborated during World War II. Maybe you participated in a group project at school or played a co-op video game with a friend. Do you think competition or collaboration is more successful in pushing you to work hard?

CHAPTER FIVE

Family Feud

A Pair No More

The Dassler brothers may have stopped talking after their split, but their rivalry kept going strong. Almost everyone in their hometown of Herzogenaurach worked for either Adidas or Puma, and the factories were located on opposite sides of a river.

The Dassler feud divided the town. The Adidas employees and Puma employees didn't socialize with each other. The shoe brand you wore determined where you went to school and where you bought groceries. Dating or marrying someone who worked for the rival company was strictly prohibited.

Herzogenaurach became known as "the town of bent necks" because the first thing people did upon meeting someone new was look down to see which brand of shoes they were wearing.

Adi and Rudolf both tried to invent the world's greatest athletic shoe and put his brother out of business. Adi never wavered from his goal of creating shoes for every type of athlete. He developed shoes for track and field athletes, football players, tennis players, boxers, bowlers, and fencers.

In the final game of the 1954 World Cup, West Germany faced Hungary. The Hungarians were heavily favored to win. In fact, they were considered the best team on

the planet. The press even called them "the Golden Team." Nobody thought the West Germans had a chance. But they had a secret weapon: their Adidas sneakers.

The day of the final game was wet and rainy. By halftime, the field was soaked. The Adidas soccer shoes were equipped with screw-on studs that could be swapped out according to different weather conditions. The team switched out their studs for extra-long ones that could dig into the soggy field and get better traction. The switch worked: West Germany won in a surprise 3–2 victory! The team was so grateful to Adi that they pulled him into their winning photo. The match would go on to earn the nickname the Mircale of Bern.

Bans and Betrayals

Even after Adi and Rudolf passed their companies along to their sons, the sneaker wars continued. Things came to a head yet again leading up to the 1968 Summer Olympics in Mexico City. Puma debuted a red sneaker with not four, or eight, but a whopping sixty-eight small spikes on each shoe. Runners began to break world records left and right.

As of
the 2020
Tokyo
Olympics,
track and
field athletes
can have up
to eleven
spikes per
shoe.

Then, two weeks before the Olympics, the international board for track and field banned the shoe. They claimed that it violated the maximum eight-spike rule. People whispered that Adidas played a role in getting the shoe off the feet of Olympic athletes and out of customers' eyes.

By the time the 1970 World Cup in Mexico came around, the rival Dassler cousins decided they had had enough of the conflict. Both wanted to sign the Brazilian soccer phenomenon Pelé, considered the greatest player in the world at the time.

Pelé helped the Brazil soccer team to FIFA World Cup victory three times: in 1958, 1962, and 1970.

GOAL!

They knew that if one of them did, that company would have a major advantage. They also knew that signing Pelé would cost an enormous amount of money and cause other players to demand more for their contracts, too. That would hurt both Adidas and Puma. So the Dasslers made an agreement called the "Pelé pact" in which both agreed not to sign the superstar. The rivalry seemed to be winding down.

The 1970 Brazilian team, led by Pelé, was one of the greatest soccer teams in history. They won game after game, until the final match of the tournament arrived. Right before the whistle blew to start the game, Pelé asked the referee to pause for a moment. The camera was trained on the soccer star, broadcasting footage all

"Innovate—
don't imitate."

—ADIDAS FOUNDER ADI DASSLER

over the world, as he bent over to tie his sneakers: Pumas.

Pact or no pact, Armin Dassler of Puma hadn't been able to resist the opportunity to see his shoes on the feet of the greatest soccer player. He had paid Pelé to wear Pumas and tie them when the timing was right. The sneaker war was back on.

The Dassler brothers' bitter feud split a family—and a town—in two. But the competition also fueled the brothers to create new and better sneaker technology. Without the rivalry, sneakers may not have been the high-tech marvels they are today.

CHAPTER SIX
The Swoosh

One morning in 1971, Bill Bowerman was eating breakfast with his wife when he had a big idea. He realized the pattern on the waffle he was eating would make the perfect grippy sole for a running shoe. Bowerman leaped up from the table and fetched two cans of liquid urethane, which was used for making shoe soles at the time. He poured them in the waffle iron and accidentally glued it shut!

Bowerman wasn't deterred, though. He kept experimenting until he had invented the first-ever waffle-soled shoe. In 1974, the Waffle Trainer hit the shelves. And it came from a small sneaker company that Bowerman had recently co-founded: Nike.

"Waffle Trainers were grabbed by the army of weekend jocks suffering from bruised feet."

—TIME MAGAZINE

Don't try this at home!

Carrying the Weight

Why was Bowerman looking for the perfect sneaker sole in the first place? To answer that question, we need to backpedal a few decades to the 1950s. At the time, Bowerman was the track and field coach at the University of Oregon. He was obsessed with sneakers. At the time, track shoes were made of heavy leather and metal. In a sport where milliseconds could mean the difference between first and second place, every bit of weight mattered. Bowerman calculated that for every ounce he could remove from a shoe, he could save his athletes from carrying the equivalent of fifty-five pounds over the course of a mile. If he could make his runners' shoes lighter, he could make his runners faster.

Bowerman wrote to footwear companies, explaining his ideas for improving their shoes. But no one listened. So he found a local cobbler to teach him how to craft shoes for himself. First, Bowerman tore apart racing shoes to figure out how they were made. Then, he experimented with new materials, such as plastic spikes, kangaroo leather, velvet, and even fish

"History is one long processional of crazy ideas."

—NIKE CO-FOUNDER PHIL KNIGHT

skin. No companies wanted to manufacture Bowerman's strange shoes. But he kept making them anyway. And one of these experiments ended up on the feet of a student athlete named Phil Knight.

The shoes that Bowerman handed Knight were strange indeed. They were handmade, with uppers constructed of the kind of rubber-coated fabric often used for wipeable tablecloths. Knight slipped them on at practice one evening, but he didn't wear them for long. His teammate Otis Davis spotted the shoes and asked to try them out. Davis liked them so much that he wore shoes that Bowerman made while training. (Davis went on to become a gold medalist in the 1960 Olympics.) It seemed like Bowerman was onto something.

After graduating from the University of Oregon and studying business at Stanford University, Knight wasn't really sure what he wanted to do next. He tried selling encyclopedias and working as an accountant. But nothing clicked, so he took off on a trip to travel the world. While Knight was visiting Japan, he spotted a pair of knockoff Adidas sneakers on display in a store. He asked the clerk which company made them. The next thing Knight knew, he was on a train headed for the Onitsuka (pronounced OH-knee-TSOO-ka) shoe factory.

Go Get 'Em, Tiger

Onitsuka Tiger had been founded by thirty-two-year-old Kihachiro Onitsuka in the aftermath of World War II, which had left Japan in ruins. Onitsuka

believed that physical activity was key to helping Japan's communities rebuild. He dreamed of making shoes for basketball, a sport that American soldiers had brought to Japan. But Onitsuka's first attempts at basketball shoes were failures. The soles were too slippery, causing players to slip and slide around on the court.

Onitsuka needed a new design idea. He found inspiration in an unexpected place: an octopus salad! According to company lore, Onitsuka was eating the dish one day

FASTER

when a tentacle's suction cup-like grippers stuck to the bowl. Onitsuka realized a basketball shoe with similar grippers on its sole would help players cling to the court. His idea became the Onitsuka Tiger 1951 OK Basketball Shoes.

Soon, Onitsuka Tiger was making all kinds of sneakers. Distance runners especially loved their Onitsuka sneakers, but they complained of blisters. Again, Kihachiro Onitsuka found inspiration in a surprising place. This time, he was taking a bath when

A Different Design

More than seventy years after Onitsuka Tiger was founded, Japanese designers are still creating some of the most inventive new sneaker designs. In 2018, fashion designer Chitose Abe teamed up with Nike to create the "Blazer with the Dunk" collection, which combined two Nike sneakers—the Blazer and the SB Dunk—into one shoe: two sets of laces, tongues, and even double swooshes!

he noticed the steamy water wrinkle his toes. He realized that heat helped blisters form, so he worked with his designers to create a shoe with perforations near the toe and sides to allow cooling air to flow in. That sneaker became the Magic Runner, released in 1960.

As the years passed, Onitsuka Tiger rolled out one new design after another. Soon, Japan's most successful athletes wore Onitsuka sneakers. When Phil Knight found his way to the Onitsuka Tiger factory, he had no idea he was stumbling into one of the most innovative sneaker companies on the planet.

Onitsuka Tiger sneakers

At first, Phil Knight sold sneakers out of the back of his car at track meets.

What's in a Name?

In 1971, Phil Knight and Bill Bowerman brainstormed a name for their original sneaker. One employee had a name come to him in a dream: Nike, after the Greek goddess of victory. But Knight didn't like it at first. He wanted to call the sneaker the sci-fi sounding "Dimension Six."

A statue of the Greek goddess Nike

Sneakers of Victory

When Knight arrived at the Onitsuka Tiger factory, the Japanese executives thought he was a high-powered businessman. Knight played along, pretending to be an American shoe importer. He got Onitsuka to agree to send him some sample shoes. Later, he secretly had to ask his father to send him money to pay for them!

Back home in the United States, Knight knew exactly who needed to see the shoes—his old coach. Bowerman liked what he saw so much, he agreed to team up with Knight to sell the shoes in the United States. They named their company Blue Ribbon Sports.

In 1971, Blue Ribbon Sports decided to end their relationship with Onitsuka Tiger and create their own shoe. It was called the Nike Cortez, with a spongy sole and a cool look—white with a red swoosh.

The Nike Cortez debuted during the 1972 Summer Olympics. Customers went wild.

Nike Cortez sneakers

Nike opened its first store in 1966 and would eventually have a presence in 170 countries throughout the world!

The Swoosh

Nike's swoosh is one of the most recognizable logos in the world, but it came from humble origins. In 1971, Phil Knight hired a graphic design student named Carolyn Davidson. Her charge for the Swoosh? $35! That fee would be worth about $257 today.

By the next year, *Runner's World* magazine was calling the Cortez "the most popular long-distance training shoe in the U.S." It proved so well-liked that Blue Ribbon Sports changed their company name to Nike, and they're still making a version of the Cortez today.

Bowerman kept churning out new designs, like sneakers with better spike placement and ones with a cushioned plate to hold the spikes.

Still, Bowerman continued to struggle with designing a shoe that could grip all kinds of surfaces, from grass to mud. That's when the Waffle Trainer came about, with a sole so grippy it didn't need spikes at all! It was an instant hit among athletes. In one year, Nike's profits nearly doubled. True to their namesake, Nike found itself with a winning shoe!

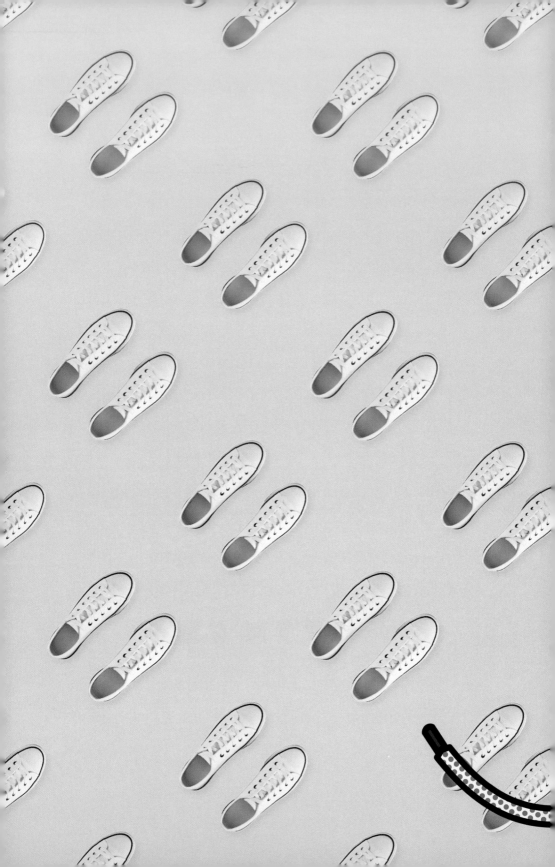

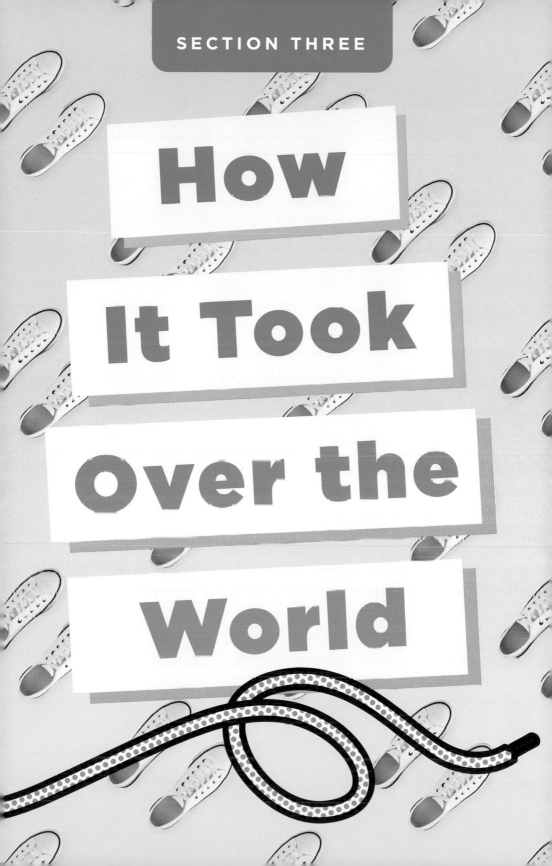

How It Took Over the World

CHAPTER SEVEN

Exercise for Everyone

Aerobics

ONE two three four, ONE two three four! Sweaty people in neon-colored spandex, wearing sweatbands and wristbands, stomped and swayed in a crowded room. It was the 1980s, and the aerobics trend was in full swing.

In 1968, a doctor named Kenneth Cooper published a book arguing a concept that was revolutionary at the time: that exercising could help keep people healthy. The book was called *Aerobics*.

Soon after, a dance teacher named Judi Sheppard Missett took

Dr. Cooper's concept, added music, and created a new type of aerobic exercise called Jazzercise. Missett led groups of women as they bopped and swayed in dance-inspired routines. In 1978, aerobics caught the attention of actress Jane Fonda. Fonda usually did ballet to exercise, but she had broken her foot while filming a movie and was looking for a new way to get fit. She

"An exercise outfit helps because it sets this time apart from the rest of your day and it makes it matter more."

—JANE FONDA

tried an aerobics class, which didn't bother her foot, and quickly became hooked.

In 1979, Fonda opened her own workout studio. Her classes quickly filled up with women. They were thrilled to have their own exercise routine and their own space in the gym, a place that had long been dominated by male bodybuilders and boxers. In 1982, Fonda shook up the exercise world even more when she released a video version of her workout routine, *Jane Fonda's Workout*.

In her video, Fonda wore a striped leotard, purple leg warmers . . . and no shoes. The sneakers that existed at the time weren't good for the sideways movements of aerobics. So people had no choice but to exercise barefoot, which made their legs and feet ache.

Most shoe companies, like Nike, brushed off aerobics and its army of side-stepping women. Instead, they focused on what they saw as "serious" athletes, such as runners and basketball players. But one company took notice. It was Reebok, a brand from

Britain trying to break into the United States sneaker market.

In 1982, Reebok released the Freestyle. It didn't look like other sneakers. It was a simple shoe made of soft leather and lined with soft terry cloth. At the top, it had two Velcro straps to support the ankle.

When Nike designers saw the Freestyle, they laughed. But when Reebok started handing out free sneakers to aerobics instructors, they loved the shoe. The first Freestyles sold out in days. Soon, Fonda was wearing them in her videos, too.

Reebok Freestyle sneaker

Off the Wall

Around the time that exercise was starting to catch on, a new extreme sport was growing more popular: skateboarding. The sport got its start in the 1950s when surfers attached metal roller-skate wheels to wooden boards. These "sidewalk surfers" rode their substitute surfboards all over California's beach towns.

At first, whether surfers were riding the ocean or the concrete, they rode barefoot.

But then they realized that skateboarding came with its unique risks. Boards often came crashing down on skaters' feet and ankles. Skaters also used their feet as brakes by dragging them along the ground. (If you've ever had a floor burn before, you know how painful that would

Vans sneakers were ideal for skaters because the shoes had extra leather material to make them more durable.

be!) They needed sturdy sneakers, and the brand they reached for was Vans.

Founded in 1966 by brothers Paul Van Doren and Jim Van Doren in Anaheim, California, the company offered to make customers shoes in any fabric and color they chose. Skaters liked Vans for their rugged canvas construction and sticky sole that helped grip the board. They also liked the company's ability to customize their orders—if they wore out one shoe faster than the other, Vans would let them buy a single replacement instead of buying a whole new pair.

In 1976, Vans released a new logo: a cartoon skateboard

emblazoned with the words "Vans 'Off the Wall.'" The slogan was a nod to the moment when a skater shot off the side of an empty swimming pool and went airborne.

The "Off the Wall" ad campaign attracted the attention of one eleven-year-old in particular. His name was Tony Hawk. After a year of begging his father to buy him a pair of Vans, young Hawk finally got his hands on some. More than seventy skateboarding championship wins later, Hawk still wears Vans.

Reebok and Vans succeeded by figuring out that it wasn't just "traditional" athletes who wanted sneakers. Anyone who wanted to get out and move wanted their own pair, too!

Skateboarding legend Tony Hawk

"You might not make it to the top, but if you are doing what you love, there is much more happiness there than being rich or famous."

—TONY HAWK

CHAPTER EIGHT

Put a Face on It

Star Power

Adidas, Puma, Nike, Reebok, Onitsuka Tiger, Keds, Vans . . . The sneaker industry was booming, but it was also becoming more and more competitive. Executives at the Converse shoe company wanted to stand out among the crowd, and they had an idea: to put the STAR into sneakers.

Chuck Taylor All Stars, also simply called Converse or Chucks, got their start as basketball shoes. When the sneaker debuted in 1917, it had a thick rubber sole and a canvas or leather upper with a star on the side. It only came in brown with black trim.

High-top Chuck Taylor All Stars

At first, sales were slow. But in 1922, the Converse company hired a salesperson that would eventually become the All Stars' namesake: Charles "Chuck" Hollis Taylor.

Chuck Taylor was a former semiprofessional basketball player. As a Converse employee,

More than one billion pairs of Converse All Stars have been sold.

Taylor traveled around the country, hosting basketball clinics to grow interest in the game; he would teach coaches and help players improve their skills. At the same time, he would convince people to wear All Stars.

As the sport of basketball evolved, All Stars evolved with it. The game got faster, and players started pivoting on the front of their feet to

Heavy Hitters

Babe Didrikson became the first woman to score an **endorsement** deal when she appeared in a 1933 car advertisement that called her the "World's Greatest Woman Athlete." Of course, she wasn't just a great female athlete; she was a great athlete, period. At the 1932 Olympics, Didrikson set world records and won gold in the javelin and the 80-meter hurdles. In her later life, she went on to dominate professional golf.

dodge and pass, so Converse added extra rubber. Later, they released a low-top version to make it easier for players to move. These new sporting features helped Converse sell more shoes.

Taylor loved the players, loved meeting coaches, and loved the game of basketball. His enthusiasm was infectious. He was so good at selling that people started ordering All Stars by asking for "Chuck Taylor's shoe." In the early 1930s, Converse made it official and added Taylor's name to the shoe's signature patch, where it remains to this day.

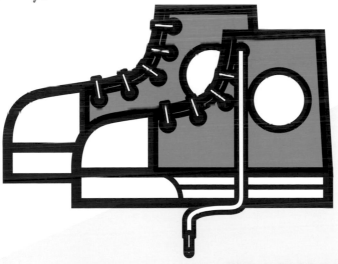

Today, three-quarters of all NBA players sport the Nike swoosh on the court.

HOW IT HAPPENED! SNEAKERS

Converse became the first sneaker company to practice the celebrity endorsement—the idea of using a well-known person to sell a product.

A Slam Dunk for Nike

In 1984, a Nike executive convinced his company that they should take all the advertising money they had and bet it all on a young basketball player named Michael Jordan. Jordan wasn't excited about an endorsement deal, though, because he preferred to wear Adidas!

Still, Nike wanted Jordan, and they promised just about anything to get him. Nike invited Jordan, along with his parents, to their headquarters in Portland, Oregon. There, they made him an unheard-of offer: Jordan would be the new face of Nike advertising. In addition to a yearly payment, he would get a percentage of every pair of shoes sold in his name as well as a small percentage of the Nike company itself. The deal was worth $2.5 million over five years (about $6 million today). That was triple any other NBA player's sneaker deal at the time! But perhaps the biggest perk was that he would get his own namesake shoe, designed especially for him.

Jordan still hesitated, but Converse and Adidas weren't offering deals like Nike. With his parents' guidance, Jordan signed on the dotted line.

Jordan debuted as a pro player for the Chicago Bulls in 1984. He was a sensation, leading his team in points, assists, rebounds, and steals. He helped the Bulls go to the playoffs. He packed the stands with screaming

Michael Jordan plays against the New Jersey Nets (now the Brooklyn Nets).

"Just Do It."

—NIKE SLOGAN, WHICH FIRST APPEARED IN A 1988 NIKE AD

fans. He won Rookie of the Year. And he did it while wearing a revolutionary new basketball shoe.

Michael Jordan's signature padded high-tops were called Air Jordans. The name was a nod to the player's habit of flying high above the court as he made dramatic dunks. Air Jordans had a logo featuring a winged basketball with a striking colorway of white, black, and red.

Air Jordans

> ## "Yo, Mike, what makes you the best player in the universe? . . . It's gotta be the shoes!"
>
> **—A COMMERCIAL CREATED BY FILMMAKER SPIKE LEE TO PROMOTE THE AIR JORDAN III SNEAKERS**

When Jordan debuted his shoes, the NBA was not happy. At the time, Converse All Stars were the official sneakers of the NBA. The rules said that every player on a team had to wear the same shoes: white sneakers accented by the team's colors. Wearing the same shoes showed a team's unity and spirit. Then Jordan stepped out on the court in shoes that said "I'm a superstar."

Jordan had to pay a $5,000 fine to the NBA, and he was told not to wear them again. Instead of feeling intimidated, though, Nike turned the NBA's outrage into great publicity. Nike encouraged Jordan to keep wearing the shoes, and the company covered the fine for each game.

Meanwhile, Nike quickly put out a new commercial. In it, the camera slowly panned down Jordan's body, focusing finally on his feet, which were covered with black censor bars. Then, the voiceover said: "On September 15, Nike created a revolutionary new basketball shoe. On October 18, the NBA threw them out of the game. Fortunately, the NBA can't stop you from wearing them. Air Jordans. From Nike."

CHA-CHING!

Air Jordans went on sale to the public on April 1, 1985, just before that season's playoffs began. They cost $65 (about $180 today), making them the most expensive basketball shoe at the time. And they came in two colorways: black and red or white and red, with a black swoosh.

Just as Jordan soared across the basketball court, the shoes flew off the shelves. Nike had hoped that its deal with Jordan would help sell $3 million worth of shoes over four years. After one year, it had sold $126 million.

Pump It Up

At the NBA All-Star Weekend in 1991, basketball player Dee Brown took a shot in the slam dunk contest. With the audience watching, he paused, then bent over and squeezed the tongues of his Reebok sneakers. He was pumping up his shoes to fill them with air! The crowd went wild . . . and Reebok's sales exploded. Talk about a successful endorsement!

All kinds of other companies jumped on the Jordan train, too. Soon, Jordan was endorsing everything from hamburgers to underwear. His Air Jordans were such a big part of his image that he even wore them in commercials for other brands.

Walking on Air

Nike's Air Jordan II sneaker hit the shelves in 1986, just in time for Jordan's second season. With sides made of faux lizard leather and a red heel, it was meant to look high fashion, and it had a hundred dollar price tag to match. But the shoe was a flop—perhaps because Jordan spent most of the season on the bench with an injury. Scared that their star would leave them for a competitor, Nike executives had to come

up with a way to make sure Jordan would stay for good.

The Air Jordan design team knew their next shoe had to be a hit. They were searching for inspiration when they came across a photo of Jordan in *Life* magazine. In the photo, Jordan soared high above the ground toward the basket, a ball in his raised left hand, his legs splayed out wide. Nike liked the photo so much that they decided to recreate it into a logo, called the Jumpman. When Nike showed Jordan, he loved it.

The Air Jordan III sneakers were revolutionary to say the least. They were the first mid-cut basketball sneaker, made of leather in an elephant skin print. The heel had a clear window to show off the air cushion inside.

Nike's Jumpman logo

The Jumpman logo, in bright red, stood out on the sneaker's tongue.

All that fame and fortune meant that Nike needed Jordan, but Jordan might not need Nike. Michael Jordan went on to create his own Jordan Brand shoe and sportswear brand.

Whether Jordan was selling shoes for his own brand or another's, one thing was for sure: Putting sneakers on famous feet sure helped them take over the world!

CHAPTER NINE

Fashion and Culture

Streetball Celebrities

In the 1970s, Rucker Park in New York City—on the corner of 155th Street and Frederick Douglass Boulevard—was the hottest venue in town for a new kind of sport: streetball.

Streetball was basketball's elbows-flying, no-holds-barred cousin. Athletes focused on their ability to perform spectacular tricks. And a player's skill at trash-talking his opponents—and entertaining the crowd— was considered almost as important as his ability to score. The best streetball players became legends, known by nicknames like Earl "The Goat" Manigault and Herman "The Helicopter" Knowings.

At the time, the New York Knicks had a point guard named Walt "Clyde" Frazier. Frazier dominated on the court, but he was perhaps best-known for his style. He would stroll around the Big Apple wearing fedoras and custom-made suits. So when Puma offered Frazier $5,000 to wear their Puma Basket—a clunky leather sneaker— Frazier wasn't interested.

With Frazier's input, Puma created a more fashionable sneaker design: lighter, more flexible, and with more padding inside. Puma covered it in suede material and added Frazier's signature. They called their new shoe the Puma Clyde. When the Knicks took the championship in 1973, many top streetball players started lacing on Clydes for games at Rucker Park. When streetball fans saw their idols wearing the new suede shoes, they wanted some, too.

Before Clydes, sneakers hadn't been for looks. They were sports shoes made to get dirty and worn. But now, kids all over the city were saving up to buy Clydes.

Once they had a pair, they treasured them. Some people checked the weather forecast before slipping into their Clydes so rain wouldn't ruin the suede material. Others carried around a toothbrush to scrub off any salt that was used to treat icy roads during the winter.

By the mid-1970s, people weren't just wearing sneakers on the basketball and streetball courts. They were wearing them everywhere! What had started out as an athletic shoe was no longer just a piece of sports equipment. Sneakers had officially made the leap from sportswear to streetwear.

Dress Code

While sneakers took the fashion world by storm, some parts of society still had their doors closed to rubber soles. Because of its history as a sports shoe, many people saw sneakers as casual footwear. Business offices, churches, and other formal places discouraged people from wearing sneakers. Fashionistas continued to step over social conventions to wear sneakers wherever they wanted. In 1969, John Lennon, a member of the legendary music band the Beatles, and artist Yoko Ono both wore white sneakers to their wedding.

In some instances, sneakers transformed themselves to become just as fancy as leather dress shoes and high heels. At first, some high fashion brands didn't take the "casual" sneaker style seriously. By 1984, though, even luxury fashion brands couldn't ignore the massive popularity of sneakers. Gucci released tennis shoes that same year—the first "luxury" sneaker, and certainly not the last. Celebrities paired their luxury sneakers with suits, dresses, and other formal attire.

While sneakers still carry a casual image today, they've made great strides to become the pair to wear everywhere, from fast food restaurants to red carpets.

Music to My Feet

About a decade after John Lennon and Yoko Ono wore white kicks to their wedding, music and sneaker culture collaborated to create the perfect pop culture moment. In the 1980s, an American hip-hop group called

Run-DMC members
from left to right:
Joseph "Run"
Simmons, Jason
"Jam Master Jay"
Mizell, and Darryl
"DMC" McDaniels

Run-DMC was bringing a fresh new sound to the music scene. The three members had a fresh new look to match: Adidas tracksuits with the signature three stripes down the side that were ideal for break-dancing. They also wore laceless three-striped Adidas Superstars, a new sneaker design with a hard shell toe.

The Superstars were such a big part of Run-DMC's look that in 1986, they released a song about them, called "My Adidas." The lyrics talk about how Run-DMC wears the shoes everywhere they go to perform at shows and rock on stage. Adidas sales shot up so fast that one company executive, named Angelo Anastasio, flew from Los Angeles to New York City to watch Run-DMC perform at Madison Square Garden and see what all the fuss was about. At the concert, the group asked everyone to hold their shoes in the air. Anastasio was astounded to see thousands of people waving around their three-striped sneakers.

Anastasio knew what he had to do. He offered the group a million-dollar

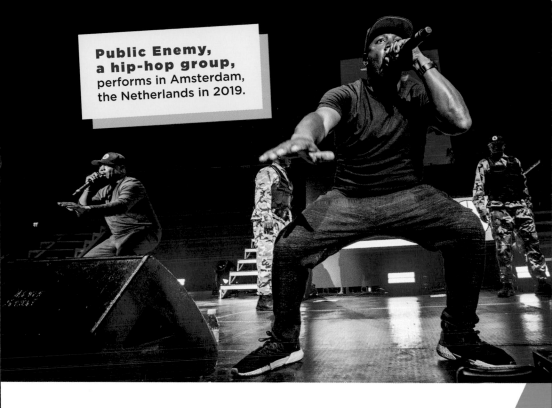

Public Enemy, a hip-hop group, performs in Amsterdam, the Netherlands in 2019.

endorsement deal. It was the first time an athletic apparel company signed a deal with stars who weren't athletes. It wasn't only basketball or tennis players who could endorse sneakers: Musicians had a huge influence on what people wore, too.

From then on, the world of rap and hip-hop was tightly tied to sneaker culture. Every time an artist wore a sneaker in

In 2021, a pair of sneakers sold at auction for $1.8 million, the highest recorded sale price for a sneaker in history.

a music video or referenced one in a song, people would go out and buy that shoe, and sales would skyrocket.

What's Old Is New Again

Most music artists took pride in keeping their sneakers fresh looking, as if they were new out of the box. But not the Beastie Boys, a rap group from Brooklyn, New York. They wore baseball caps and gold chains and scuffed sneakers. And often, those sneakers weren't the hottest new releases. Instead, they were outdated models.

The group often wore one shoe in particular: the Adidas Campus, a low-top suede shoe that the Boston Celtics basketball team had sported in 1971. In 1992, Beastie Boy Mike D wore the Campus in the cover shot of the group's album *Check Your Head.*

The Beastie Boys from left to right: Adam Yauch ("MCA"), Adam Horovitz ("Ad-Rock"), and Mike Diamond ("Mike D") in 2004.

When asked how he had gotten his hands on such an old shoe, Mike D's bandmate Ad-Rock answered, "You gotta find them, like records. It's like a hobby."

The group went on to reveal that they kept a person on staff whose entire job it was to rummage through the stockrooms of sporting goods stores, on the hunt for unworn sneakers that were no longer sold. It was a radical idea. At the time, almost nobody had even thought of wearing old sneakers. All of a sudden, the Beastie Boys made it cool!

WHAT DO YOU THINK? Sneaker fashion trends come and go. Next time you're at the store, the park, or just walking around the neighborhood, pay attention to the sneakers people are wearing. Keep count of the different colors, brands, or patterns you see. What kind of kicks are the most popular in your town right now?

CHAPTER TEN
Sneakerheads

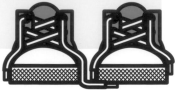

Line Up for Laces!

It was a chilly Monday in January 2016 when a customer walked up to the doors of a Jordan Brand store in Chicago, Illinois. He didn't go inside, though. He set up a folding chair and sat down. He was waiting for the release of a new Air Jordan sneaker that had quilted sides in a sandy suede color, and he wanted to be first in line. The sneaker was due to go on sale that coming Saturday . . . a full five days later!

He wasn't the only customer willing to wait. As the days went by, more and more people lined up. Some brought food. Some huddled under blankets in the cold winter weather. Some waited on behalf of

others—like one man whose nephew paid him a hundred dollars a day to hold his place in line. Some wanted to purchase the sneakers so that they could resell them later for a profit: The shoes had a sale price of $650, but online they could easily sell for $2,000 or more. And of course, some people waited in line because they wanted to own the sneakers for themselves. They were **sneakerheads,** people who collect and trade sneakers.

Sneakerheads love sneakers. They pride themselves in knowing every detail about the design and history of certain pairs of shoes. They even have their own language, with terms like beaters (dirty, scuffed sneakers), fugazi (fake), and grail (a very rare pair).

Sneakerhead culture got its start in the 1970s and 1980s, when New York City kids copied the sneakers worn by their streetball heroes. Music fans slid on their shell-toe Adidas so they could look just like their favorite group, Run-DMC, or they dug through stockrooms to find the

old Campus preferred by the Beastie Boys. Basketball fans laced up Air Jordans so they could dress like their high-flying hero.

Among sneakerheads, owning limited-edition sneakers became a status symbol. Brands took notice and began reissuing retro, or old, styles. They signed hot new players and created shoes just for them. They collaborated with celebrities. And to create even more hype, they released shoes in limited batches—just a few hundred or thousand—so that not everyone who wanted a pair could get their hands on one.

A sneaker shop in
Shibuya, Tokyo, Japan

Sneaker Culture around the Globe

Today you can find sneakerheads anywhere in the world. One of the biggest sneaker destinations is Tokyo, Japan. Sneakers have been big in Japan since the days of Onitsuka Tiger. But the sneakerhead phenomenon really took off there when Nike launched its lime–green and gray Air Max in 1995. The shoe was featured in magazines and manga, or Japanese comics. People got so

In 2021, the top five sneakers sold in the United States were all Nike-branded.

Via Vyndal is a modern pantsula dance group.

desperate to own a pair that some were willing to pay $3,000 for the honor! The Shibuya district, famous as the center of youth culture and fashion in Tokyo, is home to stores specially devoted to selling rare and exclusive sneaker models.

In South Africa, people have historically used sneakers as one way to express themselves. During the 1980s, people used

a form of dance called **pantsula** to comment on life under apartheid, a system of racial segregation in which a small minority had many more privileges than the majority. Pantsula dancers were known for their street style, and their outfits often included a pair of Converse All Stars. And South Africa's sneakerhead culture has only grown since then. In 2019, limited-edition Reeboks created in collaboration with South African rapper AKA sold out in ten minutes.

Drop It Like It's Hot

The Internet changed the sneaker world even more. Suddenly, people who wanted a special shoe had other options besides waiting in line in the cold. They could buy, sell, and trade sneakers over the Internet. They could also connect with other sneakerheads to gossip about new releases or special sales.

"Shoes are boring. Wear sneakers."

—2021 CONVERSE AD CAMPAIGN

Today, sneakerheads follow social media accounts dedicated to staying on top of the next hot sneaker drop. When they find an upcoming shoe they want, they submit applications to the store for the honor of

Eye-Catching . . . or Eww?

Some brands' limited-edition sneakers have been, well . . . odd. There have been see-through Chuck Taylors, Saucony sneakers in a colorway meant to resemble a hamburger, and even Adidas sneakers in furry fabric with a teddy bear sewn onto each sneaker's tongue.

buying the style and size they want. Then, a lottery system determines which of the lucky few actually get to trade their hard-earned dollars for the sneaker. Sometimes, customers must agree to post a photo on social media and tag the store to create even more hype for the shoes.

Sneakerheads who don't win a lottery slot can try and get their shoes secondhand. They scour websites dedicated to buying and selling sneakers. They'll often pay thousands of dollars for a special pair of kicks . . . and they risk shelling out cash for fake shoes made to look almost exactly like the real thing. Sometimes, after all that work, they miss out on the shoe they want. If that happens, there's always tomorrow when there could be news of the next hot sneaker drop.

The global sneaker market is forecasted to be worth $30 billion by 2030.

One of a Kind

One of the biggest new trends for sneakerheads is customization. Artists paint everything from superheroes to nature scenes on their client's sneakers, creating unique masterpieces. Some companies even help customers choose their own fabrics and materials to create their own custom sneakers from scratch.

Sneakers of the Future

Sneakers got their name from the shoes' ability to make footsteps so quiet. But of course, someone walking in sneakers isn't completely silent . . . not yet, anyway.

In the 2018 movie Black Panther, superhero T'Challa gets a major footwear upgrade when his superhero sister, Shuri, invents a new pair of "Sneakers" for him. Only they are no ordinary sneakers. When T'Challa steps on what appears to be just a sole, the sides and top of the shoe unfurl, covering the foot with special nanoparticles. Then, Shuri says, "I made them completely sound-absorbent."

This piece of movie fiction caught the attention of YouTuber Jake Laser, known for his real-life versions of movie props. When fans begged him to make the Black Panther Sneakers next,

Laser agreed. In his search for the perfect sound-absorbing material, Laser tried out leather, socks, and memory foam. But none of them were quiet enough. Then, he discovered aerogel. Invented in the 1930s and extensively researched by NASA, aerogel is the world's lightest solid, a spongy structure made up of 99.8 percent air. Extremely durable, lightweight, and a powerful insulator, it's the ultimate material for surviving space missions. And it's also extremely sound-absorbent.

Laser outfitted a shoe with aerogel and tested it out. He measured the loudness of his silent sneakers with a decibel meter and found that their footfalls couldn't be heard over normal background noise, making them essentially silent. Now that's a super shoe!

The kids' sneaker industry in the U.S. sold nearly 125 percent more sneakers in 2021 than in 2020!

What will the sneakers of the future be like? They won't just be super silent. Innovators around the world are hard at work designing sneakers with all kinds of mind-bending features. The ShiftWear sneaker has an HD color display on its side that links to a smartphone, allowing the wearer to change the shoe's design with the touch of a button. DigitSole can track the wearer's movements, calories burned, impact force, and more, to give athletes and everyday people instant feedback on their performance. They'll even heat your feet if you're cold!

Nike has also released sneakers that can lace up by themselves. Self-tightening technology helps create more adaptive, inclusive footwear for everyone, regardless of whether they are physically able to bend over to tie their shoes.

Far from their beginnings as equipment for athletes, sneakers have become far more than just shoes. They're status symbols for sports fans. They're holy grails for collectors. And with all the new sneaker innovations on the horizon, who knows what kind of shoes you'll be slipping on in the future. You might even be the one who invents the next big sneaker!

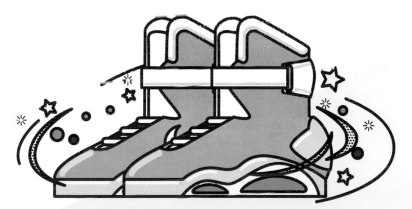

A Pumped-Up Timeline

7000 BCE

Indigenous people in modern-day Oregon wear sandals made with a plant called sagebrush.

776 BCE

The first known Olympic Games takes place in ancient Greece.

1839 CE

Charles Goodyear discovers vulcanization by accidentally throwing rubber onto a hot stove.

Shoemakers working in present-day Myanmar in the late 1800s

1860s

The first sneakers with vulcanized rubber soles are made.

1916

Keds launches.

1917

The All Stars sneaker is released by Converse.

1936	1948	1949	1951
Jesse Owens blows away the Olympic competition wearing a pair of sneakers created by the Dassler brothers.	Puma is founded.	Adidas is founded.	The Onitsuka Tiger basketball shoes, inspired by octopus grippers, go on sale.

Classic Puma, Nike,
and Adidas sneakers

1966	1968	1970s	1971
Vans is founded.	Dr. Kenneth Cooper publishes *Aerobics*.	Streetball takes off.	Nike's Bill Bowerman invents the waffle sole.

1972

The Nike Cortez debuts.

1982

Jane Fonda releases her first workout video. Reebok releases the Freestyle aerobics sneaker.

1984

Nike signs a historic endorsement deal with Michael Jordan.

1986

Run-DMC releases the hip-hop hit "My Adidas."

Today, Nike sells about 900 million items every year!

1988

The Air Jordan III sports the first Jumpman logo.

1992

The Beastie Boys feature an old pair of Adidas Campus sneakers on their album cover.

2021

The kids' sneaker industry in the U.S. grows by nearly 25 percent from 2020.

Shoe It Yourself!

The sensational story of sneakers is one that involves creativity, ambition, and savvy advertising skills. Get your own innovation bubbling with these activities!

Cook Up an Idea

Bill Bowerman's breakfast waffles inspired him to create a new sneaker sole. Look in your kitchen to see if inspiration strikes you, too. Maybe it's a new idea for a food product, a new cooking utensil, or something else entirely.

Design a Logo

The signature Nike Swoosh and Jordan's Jumpman logo helped create a loyal following for Nike sneakers. Choose two items that you own—it could be clothes, books, food, or something else. Draw a logo that you think will connect the two items together.

Your Dream Sneaker

What kind of sneakers would you like to own in the future? What would they look like? Would they have special technology like the auto-lacing sneakers? Don't forget to give your "dream" future sneaker a cool name!

Glossary

Aerobics: A rhythmic physical exercise, usually set to music

Croquet: A sport where mallets are used to hit balls through hoops stationed in a grassy field

Endorsement: The act of supporting or promoting something

Latex: A milky fluid that is found in plants and trees

Pantsula: A dance tradition founded in South Africa

Sneakerhead: Someone who loves and knows a lot about sneakers

Streetball: An informal variation of basketball where individual players' showmanship is valued

Synthetic: Artificial, or human-made

Vulcanization: A way of hardening rubber by combining it with sulfur and heating it

Note: Some of these words may have more than one meaning. These definitions match what the words mean in this book.

Index

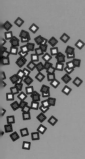